First World War
and Army of Occupation
War Diary
France, Belgium and Germany

17 DIVISION
Divisional Troops
34 Sanitary Sections
28 June 1915 - 31 March 1917

WO95/1997/2

The Naval & Military Press Ltd
www.nmarchive.com
Published in association with The National Archives

Published by

The Naval & Military Press Ltd

Unit 10 Ridgewood Industrial Park,

Uckfield, East Sussex,

TN22 5QE England

Tel: +44 (0) 1825 749494

www.naval-military-press.com

www.nmarchive.com

This diary has been reprinted in facsimile from the original. Any imperfections are inevitably reproduced and the quality may fall short of modern type and cartographic standards.

© Crown Copyright
Images reproduced by permission of The National Archives, London, England, 2015.

Contents

Document type	Place/Title	Date From	Date To
Heading	WO95/1997/2		
Heading	17th Division 34th Sanitary Section Jun 1915-Mar 1917 To 5 Army		
Heading	17th Division Summary but not copied 34th Sanitary Section. Vol I June To Oct 15 Dec 16		
Heading	War Diary of No 34 Sanitary Section 17th Division From 28th June 1915 to 31st October 1915 Vol I		
War Diary	London	28/06/1915	28/06/1915
War Diary	Winchester	29/06/1915	15/07/1915
War Diary	Havre	16/07/1915	16/07/1915
War Diary	Lumbres	17/07/1915	17/07/1915
War Diary	Renescure	18/07/1915	18/07/1915
War Diary	Steenvoorde	19/07/1915	21/07/1915
War Diary	Reninghelst	24/07/1915	04/10/1915
War Diary	Steenvoorde	07/10/1915	21/10/1915
War Diary	Ouderdom	22/10/1915	23/10/1915
War Diary	G 15 C 5.9	24/10/1915	31/10/1915
Heading	17th Division 34th San. Sect Vol 2 Summarised but not copied Nov 1915		
Heading	War Diary of No 34 Sanitary Section 17th Division From 1st to 30th November 1915 Volume II.		
War Diary	Sheet 28 G15.c. 5.9	01/11/1915	30/11/1915
Miscellaneous	Appendix I	11/11/1915	11/11/1915
Heading	17th Div Summarised but not copied Dec 1915 34th San. Sect. Vol 3		
Heading	War Diary of No 34 Sanitary Section 17th Division From 1st to 31st December 1915 Vol III		
War Diary	Sheet 28 G 15c 5.9	01/12/1915	31/12/1915
Heading	San. Sect. 34 Vol 4 Jan 16 Div.17 Jan 1916		
Heading	War Diary of No 34 Sanitary Section 17th Divn From 1st to 31st Jany 1916 vol IV		
War Diary	Sheet 28 G 15c 5.9	01/01/1916	31/01/1916
Heading	34 San. Sect 17th Div Vol 5 Feb 1916		
Heading	War Diary of No 34 Sanitary Section 17th Division. From 1st to 29th February 1916. Vol. V		
War Diary		01/02/1916	29/02/1916
Heading	War Diaries of No. 34. Sanitary Sections-17th Division For the months of March and April 1916		
Heading	War Diary of No 34 Sanitary Section 17th Division From 1st to 31st March. 1916. Vol. VI. 34 San Sep Vol. 6		
War Diary		01/03/1916	31/03/1916
Heading	War Diary of No 34 Sanitary Section 17th Division From 1st to 31st April 1916 Vol VII		
War Diary		01/04/1916	30/04/1916
Miscellaneous			
Heading	War Diary of 34th Sanitary Section 17th Division From 1st May to 31st May 1916 Vol. VIII 34 San Sect Vol 8		
War Diary	C.25 A.5.C. Sheet 36	01/05/1916	31/05/1916

Heading	17th Division Confidential War Diary of 34th Sanitary Section 17th Division From 1st June To 30th June 1916 Volume IX 34 San Sec Vol 9		
War Diary		01/06/1916	30/06/1916
Heading	War Diary of 34th Sanitary Section 17th Division From 1st July to 31st July 1916. Volume X 34 San Sic Vol 10		
War Diary		01/07/1916	31/07/1916
Heading	War Diary Of 34th Sanitary Section 17th Division From 1st August To 31st August 1916 Volume XI 34 San Sec Vol II		
War Diary		01/08/1916	31/08/1916
Heading	19th Div. No. 34 Sanitary Section Sept 1916		
Heading	War Diary of 34th Sanitary Section 17th Divn From 1st to 30th September 1916 Volume X		
War Diary		01/09/1916	30/09/1916
Heading	War Diary of 34th Sanitary Section 17th Divn from 1st to 31st October 1916 Vol XI		
War Diary		01/10/1916	31/10/1916
Heading	17th Div Vol 14 War Diary of 34th Sanitary Section from 1st to 30th November 1916 Vol XII		
War Diary		01/11/1916	30/11/1916
Heading	17th Div Vol 15 War Diary of 34th Sanitary Section from 1st to 31st Dec-1916 Vol XIII		
War Diary		01/12/1916	31/12/1916
Heading	17th Div Vol 16 War Diary of 34th Sanitary Section from 1st to 31st January 1917 Volume		
War Diary		01/01/1917	31/01/1917
Heading	17th Div Vol 17 War Diary of 34th Sanitary Section. from 1st to 28th Feby. 1917. Volume		
War Diary		01/02/1917	28/02/1917
Heading	17th Div Vol 18 War Diary of 34th Sanitary Section from 1st to 31st. March 1917. Volume XVI		
War Diary	Heilly	01/03/1917	01/03/1917
War Diary	Contay	02/03/1917	10/03/1917
War Diary	Talmas	10/03/1917	31/03/1917

W995/1997(2)1997(2) sign

17TH DIVISION

34TH SANITARY SECTION

JUN 1915 - ~~DEC 1916~~
MAR 1917

To 5 ARMY

121/7593

17th Hussars

Summarised but not copied

34th Sanitary Section
Vol I

June to Oct 15

Jan 16

CONFIDENTIAL

War Diary
of
No 34 Sanitary Section
17th Division

from 28th June 1915 to 31st October 1915

VOL I

Army Form C. 2118

PAGE I

WAR DIARY
or
INTELLIGENCE SUMMARY

(Erase heading not required.)

Instructions regarding War Diaries and Intelligence Summaries are contained in F. S. Regs., Part II. and the Staff Manual respectively. Title Pages will be prepared in manuscript.

Place	Date	Hour	Summary of Events and Information	Remarks and references to Appendices
LONDON	28.6.15	2 p.m	Received orders to join 17th Division at E. Arnold to Burnley Court, WINCHESTER.	Sheldon Lt R.A.M.C
WINCHESTER	29.6.15	12.30 p	Arrived at WINCHESTER. Quartered by D.A.D.M.S. (Major Woolley) at Camp at Hursley, for the Beavey R.A.M.C	
"	30.6.15		Attached to 3rd Rutlandshire Fusiliers for rations, doctors engaged in camp inspection, creation of	
"	1.7.15		Camp incinerators, instructing Regt. Sanitary Duty Men in their work.	
"	12.7.15	8 a.c.	Left Hursley Camp, marched to SOUTHAMPTON, boarded transport "Blackwell" at 12.30 p.m. Left Southampton at 9 p.m	Pte E.G. Parker 13.7.15
HAVRE	13.7.15	3 am	Arrived at HAVRE. Then Quartiers Dept marched by train at 10.30 p.m. Took Lorry + horses by to road at 8.30 p.m with ahead + equipment.	
LUMBRES	14.7.15	7.30 pm	Arrived at LUMBRES. Billeted for night in town.	
RENESCURE	15.7.15		Marched to RENESCURE. Billeted for night in schoolroom. Motor lorry & mail return	
STEENVOORDE	17.7.15		Marched to STEENVOORDE. Billets in barn on east side of town.	
"	18.7.15 22.7.15		Sections engaged in sanitary improvement of Billets & Camp in Steenvoorde area occupied by troops of 17th Division	Lt Robertson Lt R.A.M.C to Lt Beavey R.A.M.C

WAR DIARY or INTELLIGENCE SUMMARY

Army Form C. 2118
PAGE II

Place	Date	Hour	Summary of Events and Information	Remarks and references to Appendices
RENINGHELST	25/7/15		Marched to RENINGHELST. Billeted in chapel in village. J. Richardson W/O A.M.C. for the Benny Ridge. Section engaged in daily inspection of area occupied by 14th Divisional Troops. JR.	
"	26/7/15		8 a.m. of section posted to duty on water supplies. 8 men engaged digging hole & frame will stand for fly trap. Arranged with S.S.O. (sup. Quota) to take over the distribution of disinfectants to the troops of the Division. JR	
"	27/7/15		Group Inspection & other sanitary arranged. Sweeping & cleaning & disinfecting of public & house sanitary conveniences engaged in. JR. Routine work continued. JR.	
"	28/7/15		Routine work & disinfection of reservoir blankets by steam & short portable disinfector started. JR.	
"	29/7/15		Routine work. 2 men posted to water supply duty at MONT DES CATS. JR.	
"	30/7/15		Routine work & disinfection of blankets continued. J. Richardson W/O R.A.M.C for the Benny Ridge	

WAR DIARY
or
INTELLIGENCE SUMMARY
(Erase heading not required.)

Army Form C. 2118

PAGE III

Place	Date	Hour	Summary of Events and Information	Remarks and references to Appendices
RICHEBOURG ST	1/8/15 2/8/15		Routine work continued. Application to R.A.M.C. for 3" Beeney Ream.	
	3/8/15		Pte SKINNER 2491 applying for Admission was removed to Hospital & counted. J.R.	
	4/8/15		2 men attached to 2nd Infantry Brigade for sanitary information & visits. J.R.	
	5/6/15		Routine work continued. J.R.	
	10/8/15			
	11/8/15		2 men engaged storing equipment etc from Mont Grisoux. J.R.	
	20/8/15		Routine work continued. J.R.	
	21/8/15		Return Affects Paynte, Awards 5 Hospital supplies for Adv Estaches. J.R.	
	22/8/15		Routine work continued. J.R.	
	23/8/15		asking Appect. approval resumed & Duty Application to R.A.M.C. for St Beeney Reame	
	24/8/15		Routine work continued. J.R.	
	31/8/15			

Army Form C. 2118

PAGE IV

WAR DIARY
or
INTELLIGENCE SUMMARY
(Erase heading not required.)

Instructions regarding War Diaries and Intelligence Summaries are contained in F. S. Regs., Part II. and the Staff Manual respectively. Title Pages will be prepared in manuscript.

Place	Date	Hour	Summary of Events and Information	Remarks and references to Appendices
RENINGHELST	1/9/15		Routine work continued. J.Richardson Lt.R.a.m.c. for 4 Berry R.a.m.c.	
"	8/9/15		Lieut Berry Offr. dest. sick. Lieut Foley, 52nd Field Ambulance Offr. for him. J.R.	
"	9/9/15 10/9/15		Routine Work. J.R.	
"	11/9/15 12/9/15		Moving + disinfecting of equipment opened 5 foot + mouth Disease (Rt hut 27. R.2.C.) J.R.	
"	13/9/15		Lieut Berry returned to duty. J.R.	
"	14/9/15 15/9/15		Clothes found to infection of R.2.C. hospitals in shed disinfector J.R.	
"	16/9/15 17/9/15		Routine Work. J.R.	
"	20/9/15 21/9/15		Lieut Berry Offr sick (rheumatism). Lieut Cotter 31st Field Ambulance acting Temporary Offr. J.R.	
"	24/9/15		Routine Work.	
"	25/9/15 26/9/15 27/9/15 28/9/15		J.Richardson Lieut. R.A.M.C. for A. Costen R.A.M.C.	

Army Form C. 2118

PAGE V

WAR DIARY
or
INTELLIGENCE SUMMARY
(Erase heading not required.)

Instructions regarding War Diaries and Intelligence Summaries are contained in F.S. Regs., Part II and the Staff Manual respectively. Title Pages will be prepared in manuscript.

Place	Date	Hour	Summary of Events and Information	Remarks and references to Appendices
REMINGHELST	1/10/15		Sent to Refuge Road Up section vice Lieut Carter. Yphoclerken follows to Re Red Renne	
"	2/10/15		Routine work. JR.	
"	3/10/15 4/10/15			
"	5/10/15	11 a.m.	Moved to STEENVOORDE with Divisional Headquarters. Men billeted in town. Came into of town. JR.	
STEENVOORDE	7/10/15		Routine work. JR.	
"	13/10/15			
"	8/10/15		Inspection of clothing & equipment of no 1 C B'ty a Mount Broene at 99th Brigade R.F.A. JR.	
"	16/10 17/10/15		Routine work. JR	
"	18/10/15		Inspection of equipment in specal C posts a Mount Broene & "C" B'ty 80th Brigade R.F.A	
"	20/10/15		Routine work. JR	

WAR DIARY or INTELLIGENCE SUMMARY

Army Form C. 2118

PAGE VI

Place	Date	Hour	Summary of Events and Information	Remarks and references to Appendices
STEENVOORDE	21/10/15		Capt. Bloomworth & proceeded to Ouderdom (8.15 p.m.) Attached to 3rd Field Ambulance	
OUDERDOM	22/10/15		Approved provision of helping camp. JR	Abelaker scheme for N. Red Farm
"	23/10/15		Moved to G.15.c.5.9. (N.p.of 28) & proceeded with sanitary supervision of Divisional area. Posted 1 NCO & 1 bn to Water Tanks at H.14.a. & 1 NCO. & skelpipe at H.22.a. Fatigue men of 3rd Division continued on duties at Coventry at H.11.D.9.14. Water Tanks at H.14.a. & skelpipe at H.22.a. as well as incinerator (Mc) at G.16.a.3.4. JR	
G.15.c.5.9	24/10/15		Routine work. JR.	
"	25/10/15		1 N.C.O. & 1 am party for sanitary duties at Reninghelst (Divisional Headqrs) arrived by fatigue man (10) JR	

WAR DIARY
or
INTELLIGENCE SUMMARY

Army Form C. 2118

PAGE VII

Place	Date	Hour	Summary of Events and Information	Remarks and references to Appendices
G.15.c.5.9.	26/10/15		Routine work. J.Richardson to Rouen to see Reid Reeve.	
"	27/10/15		Nos. 2564 Sgt. Bulley detailed to represent the Unit at inspection of troops at Reninghelst by His Majesty THE KING. JR.	
"	28/10/15 29/10/15		Routine work. JR	
"	30/10/15		Lieut J. Richardson off to Ten vice Lieut Reid	
"	31/10/15		Fatigue men & 3rd Division relieved to fatigue men of 14th Division.	

J Richardson Lieut RAMC

34th Lan: Sec.
vol: 2

$\frac{124}{7624}$

17th Burscum

Summoned but not cited

S
Nov 1915

Nov 15.

CONFIDENTIAL

WAR DIARY

of

No 34 SANITARY SECTION

— 17th DIVISION —

from 1st to 30th November 1915 —

VOLUME II.

WAR DIARY or INTELLIGENCE SUMMARY

Army Form C. 2118
Page 1

Place	Date	Hour	Summary of Events and Information	Remarks and references to Appendices
SHEET 28 G.15.c.5.9	4/1/15		Routine work continued. J. Richardson Lieut. R.A.M.C.	
	5/1/15		Lieut. G.R. Matthews R.A.M.C.(J). Posted to the section under instruction with a view to taking over command. J.R.	
"	6/1/15			
"	7/1/15		Routine work continued. J.R.	
"	12/1/15		Lieut Matthews took over administration of 17th Divisional Baths in Potinjze for Capt Boyd. Appendix I	
"	11/1/15		3rd Field Ambulance. J.R.	
"	12/1/15		Routine work continued. J.R.	
"	13/1/15			
"	14/1/15			
"	15/1/15		Lt. Richardson handed over command of the section to Lt. Matthews R.A.M.C.(T) J.R.	

WAR DIARY or INTELLIGENCE SUMMARY

Army Form C. 2118

PAGE II

Place	Date	Hour	Summary of Events and Information	Remarks and references to Appendices
SHEET 28 G.15.c.6.9.	15/11/15		Lieut. E.R. Matthews, R.A.M.C.(T) took over control of Sanitary Section this date.	ERM
"	16/11/15		Routine work continued. (Sanitary work, and administration of 17th Divisional Batts.)	ERM
"	17/11/15 to 20/11/15		" also engaged with the construction of Sanitary Conveniences at Y.M.C.A. G.17.c. Sheet 28. and administration of 17th Divl. Batts.	ERM
"	21/11/15 to 22/11/15		" and work at 17th Divl. Batts	ERM
"	23/11/15		" (Sanitary work, and work at Batts), and spraying 55 huts, vacated by 3rd Cavalry Division (digging party) at H.14.c. Sheet 28.	ERM
"	24/11/15 to 30/11/15		" (Sanitary work, and work at 17th Divl. Batts).	ERM

E.R.Matthews
Lt. R.A.M.C.

WAR DIARY or INTELLIGENCE SUMMARY

Army Form C. 2118.

(Erase heading not required.)

Hour, Date, Place | **Summary of Events and Information** | **Remarks and references to Appendices**

APPENDIX 1

On November 11th 1915 the management of 17th Division Battns Laundry at Poperinghe was transferred to No 34 Sanitary Section 17th Divn from the 52nd Field Amb. Capt Dougal of the latter handing over the charge of the establishment to Lieut E.R. Matthews R.A.M.C. o/c No 34 SANITARY SECTN

At the time of transfer there were employed in the Battns 27 men and 57 women, but this number is insufficient and will be increased at an early date. The arrangement regarding the running of the Baths and Laundry is as follows:—

Batches of men are sent from the trenches, or from various units, for bathing, their soiled underclothing is put into large canvas bags at the baths, and after these men have had their bath a clean set of underclothing is given to each man in exchange for the dirty set. While the men are having their bath 6 women are engaged at the laundry ironing the seams of the mens' Khaki clothing to kill lice. The dirty underclothing is first put into boiling water to which Creol and Paraffin oil is added so then disinfected in a "Perish" portable disinfector on the premises; it is then washed out at the laundry, passed on to a wringing room where 12 women are employed in darning socks and in mending the shirts &c

ERM

(Stamp: 34th SANITARY SECTION 30.XI.15 17th Division R.A.M.C. (T))

WAR DIARY
or
INTELLIGENCE SUMMARY

PAGE 2.

(Erase heading not required.)

APPENDIX I contd:-

In addition to the useful work just described, men coming from the trenches and from various units overnight and going on leave by the 5 A.M. train are accommodated in the large rooms over the laundry. They are provided with sleeping accommodation; their clothing if wet is dried and they are given light refreshments such as Coffee, Cocoa & Biscuits before proceeding to their train. A buffet is now being established and arrangements have been made for the supply of magazines, books &c for their use. Officers going on leave are also provided with a bedroom with breakfast. The same applies to Officers & men arriving back from leave overnight & proceeding to their units in the morning. A shed is being erected to accommodate the officers horses, and a large shed is now in course of erection for the men to occupy while waiting their train for a Batt.

A stock of new clothing is kept on the premises so that where a man's clothing is beyond repair he may with the approval of the O/c of Batt or the N.C.O. i/c have new clothing provided.

E.R. Matthews
Lt R A M C
O/c 17th Div. Batt.

24th Jan: Sect,
Vol: 3

12/7935.

17 k /

F/256/1

Summaries but not copied

S
Dec 1915

CONFIDENTIAL

War Diary
of
No 34 Sanitary Section
17th Division
From 1st to 31st December 1915

Vol III.

Army Form C. 2118.

WAR DIARY
or
INTELLIGENCE SUMMARY

(Erase heading not required.)

PAGE 7.

34th SANITARY SECTION
R.A.M.C. (T)

Instructions regarding War Diaries and Intelligence Summaries are contained in F. S. Regs., Part II. and the Staff Manual respectively. Title pages will be prepared in manuscript.

Hour, Date, Place	Summary of Events and Information	Remarks and references to Appendices
8 P.M Sheet 28 C 15 c S.9 6/12/15 to 12/12/15	Routine Work	Note :– The expression "Routine Work" refers to General Sanitary Supervision of the area and billets occupied by troops of the 17th Div. Batt.) in addition to the ordinary work of inspection, the disinfection of huts; incineration of refuse and faeces (in 3 built incinerators now shortly under construction); control of the Sanitary Testing of the Water Supply, its renewal chlorination, to keep of records and control of the supplies at H 14 A and H 22 A Sheet 28, more also
8 P.M 13/12/15	Routine Work. Administration of 17th Div Batt. transferred to Capt DOUGAL of the 52nd FIELD AMBULANCE.	
8 P.M 13/12/15 to 31/12/15	Routine Work.	

E.R.McArthur Lt. R.A.M.C.

1247 W.3290 200,000 (E) 8/14 J.B.C.&A. Forms/C.2118/11.

WAR DIARY
or
INTELLIGENCE SUMMARY

(Erase heading not required.)

Army Form C. 2118.

PAGE II

Hour, Date, Place	Summary of Events and Information	Remarks and references to Appendices
		under the management of this Unit, an area the Cemetery at H XI D 9.4 Sheet 28. To each of the Infantry Brigades a man of the Sanitary Section is permanently attached, and at Desvres Heights 2 men of the Unit are permanently on duty. In addition to the Sanitary Section as provided for with WAR ESTABLISHMENT, 35 men on the average were attached for fatigue duties, this number being mostly composed of temporarily unfit for duty with their own units.

E.R. Mockhurst Lt. R.A.M.C.
O.C. Sanitary Section,
17th Division 31/12/15.

F/256/2.

San: Sect: 34
Vol: 4
Jan 16

17

17 Div

Jan 1916

CONFIDENTIAL

War Diary
of
No 34 Sanitary Section
17th Divn

From 1st to 31st Jany 1916

Vol IV

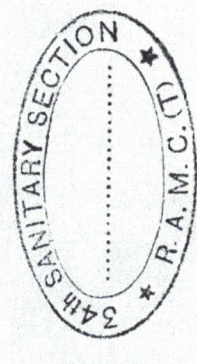

Army Form C. 2118.

PAGE I

WAR DIARY
INTELLIGENCE SUMMARY

Hour, Date, Place	Summary of Events and Information	Remarks and references to Appendices
Sheet 28 G15c 5.9 1/1/16 to 6/1/16 E.R.M.	Routine work, and inspecting Camps occupied by 17th Division	(See Vol. III re- definition of "Routine Work".
6/1/16 E.R.M.	Left Section Headqtrs at G15c 5.9 POPERINGHE at 9am (Sheet 28) entrained at Poperinghe St Omer arrived ST OMER 1 pm. Proceeded by road to Telegon TILQUES Took over billets vacated by the Sanitary Section of 24th Division. Map reference R.14.c.9.1 Sheet 27 A. S.E. Stores and equipment conveyed by road in motor lorry.	

E.R.M.

Army Form C. 2118.

PAGE II

WAR DIARY
INTELLIGENCE SUMMARY
(Erase heading not required.)

Hour, Date, Place	Summary of Events and Information	Remarks and references to Appendices
7/1/16 to 31/1/16	Routine work, and inspecting billets in Rest Area, also disinfecting blankets in use by Divisional troops; about 12,000 blankets collected from various units, conveyed to the disinfector, disinfected, and returned the same day to Units. In addition to "Routine work", a variety of model incinerators, grease traps, latrines, urine pits and other sanitary appliances were constructed for inspection by those attending the Technical School General, and those attending. E.R. Matthews Lt. R.A.M.C. O/C 34th Sanitary Section 17th Division	

84. Sam. Sget
17 ᴀ 3 is
Vol. 5

Feb 1916

CONFIDENTIAL

War Diary

of

No. 34 Sanitary Section

17th Division.

From 1st to 29th February, 1916.

Vol. V

Army Form C. 2118.

WAR DIARY
or
INTELLIGENCE SUMMARY

(Erase heading not required.)

Instructions regarding War Diaries and Intelligence Summaries are contained in F.S. Regs., Part II. and the Staff Manual respectively. Title pages will be prepared in manuscript.

Hour, Date, Place	Summary of Events and Information	Remarks and references to Appendices
1/2/16 to 5/2/16	Routine work and inspecting camps occupied by the 17th Division. Headquarters of Unit R.14.C.9.1 Sheet 27A. S.E.	(See Vol III re-Definition of "Routine work"). E.R.M.
6/2/16	Proceeded by motor lorry with 6 men to RENINGHELST to take over duties from 3rd Division. Posted relieving men to duties, ie, Div. Baths, 2 men to Water Temporarily i/c and 2 at G.34.C.7.3 Sheet 28 duty at L.32.B.8.7 Sheet 27.A. Returned by motor to TILQUES.	E.R.M.
7/2/16 to 8/2/16	Clearing up before removal. Unit and attached men left TILQUES at 9.15 a.m., and proceeded by train from STOMER to GODEWAERSVELDE. Marched to RENINGHELST, arrived 5 p.m. Headquarters of Unit G 34 Sheet 28.	E.R.M.
9/2/16 to 29/2/16	Routine work, and inspecting camps occupied by the 17th Division, and those temporarily attached to the 17th Division.	E.R.M.

E.R. Matthews
Capt. R.A.M.C.(T)
O/c 34th Sanitary Section,
17th Division.

WAR DIARES

of

No.34. Sanitary Sections - 17th Division

For the months of March and April 1916

34 San Sp
Vol. 6

CONFIDENTIAL

WAR DIARY
of
No. 34 SANITARY SECTION
17th DIVISION

FROM 1st to 31st MARCH, 1916.

Vol. VI.

Army Form C. 2118.

WAR DIARY
or
INTELLIGENCE SUMMARY

(Erase heading not required.)

Instructions regarding War Diaries and Intelligence Summaries are contained in F. S. Regs., Part II. and the Staff Manual respectively. Title pages will be prepared in manuscript.

Hour, Date, Place	Summary of Events and Information	Remarks and references to Appendices
1/3/16 to 7/3/16	Routine work at RENINGHELST G 34 Sheet 28.	(see Vol III, re-definition of "Routine work"). ERM
8/3/16	Section proceeded with fatigue men to STEENVOORDE K 31 - D - 37 Sheet 27.	ERM
9/3/16	Routine work at STEENVOORDE	ERM
10/3/16	Section proceeded with fatigue men from STEENVOORDE K 31. D. 3.7 Sheet 27 to MERRIS F.1.D 1.3 Sheet 36.A	ERM
11/3/16 20/3/16	Routine work at MERRIS.	ERM
21/3/16	O/C proceeded with advance party to take over duties from Sanitary Section 21st Division at ARMENTIÈRES C.25. A.S.C. Section stores and attached fatigue men being transferred from the MERRIS to ARMENTIÈRES.	ERM
22/3/16 23/3/16 to 31/3/16	Transfer of Section from MERRIS to ARMENTIÈRES completed. Routine work at ARMENTIÈRES.	ERM

E.R.Matthews
Capt. R.A.M.C.(T)
O/C 34th Sanitary Sec. 17th Division

34 San Coy
Vol 7

CONFIDENTIAL

War Diary
of
No 34 Sanitary Section
17th Division
From 1st To 31st April 1916

Vol VII

WAR DIARY
or
INTELLIGENCE SUMMARY

(Erase heading not required.)

Army Form C. 2118.

Hour, Date, Place	Summary of Events and Information	Remarks and references to Appendices
1/4/16 to 30/4/16	Routine work at ARMENTIÈRES C.25. A.S.C.	S.R.M. "Routine Work" include:- ① Inspection of billets occupied by the troops. ② Cleaning of drains at ARMENTIÈRES & PONT NIEPPE. ③ Removal of refuse from billets and from houses occupied by civilian population. ④ Incineration of and refuse. ⑤ Cleaning of Cesspits. ⑥ Periodic testing of water from wells. S.R.M. J.R. Matthews Capt. R.A.M.C. (T) O/c 3⁴ᵗʰ Sanitary Sec. 17ᵗʰ Division

Army Form C. 2118.

WAR DIARY
or
INTELLIGENCE SUMMARY
(Erase heading not required.)

Instructions regarding War Diaries and Intelligence Summaries are contained in F. S. Regs., Part II. and the Staff Manual respectively. Title pages will be prepared in manuscript.

Hour, Date, Place	Summary of Events and Information	Remarks and references to Appendices
		(7) Disinfection of infected billets.
		(8) General supervision of the area occupied by the Division.
		(9) Supervision of the burial of horses.
		(10) Cleaning of drains.
		For the purpose of carrying out this work the town of ARMENTIÈRES is divided into districts, civilian carts are also hired.
		E R Matthews
Capt. R.A.M.C. (T.)
O/c. 3th Sanitary Sec
17th Division

1247 W 3299 200,000 (E) 8/14 J.B.C. & A. Forms/C. 2118/11.

34.San.teet
Vol R

CONFIDENTIAL

WAR DIARY
OF
34th Sanitary Section
17th DIVISION

FROM 1st MAY to 31st MAY 1916

VOL. VIII

Army Form C. 2118.

WAR DIARY
or
INTELLIGENCE SUMMARY
(Erase heading not required.)

Instructions regarding War Diaries and Intelligence Summaries are contained in F. S. Regs., Part II. and the Staff Manual respectively. Title pages will be prepared in manuscript.

Hour, Date, Place	Summary of Events and Information	Remarks and references to Appendices
1/5/16 to 10/5/16 C.25.A.5.C. Sheet 36.	Routine work at ARMENTIÈRES	"Routine work" is as set out in Vol. VII.
11/5/16 to 13/5/16	Handing over to N.Z. Div.; relieved on 13th.	
14/5/16	Accompanied lorry with Stores and men, and proceeded to training Area at TILQUES R.14.C.9.1. Sheet 27 A.S.E.	
15/5/16 to 31/5/16	Routine work at TILQUES	"Routine work" is as set out in Vol III

E R Matthews
Capt RAMC (T)
O/C 34th San Sec.
17th Div.

34 San Sec
Vol E
9

14th Division

CONFIDENTIAL

WAR DIARY
OF
34th SANITARY SECTION
17th DIVISION

FROM 1st JUNE TO 30th JUNE 1916

VOLUME IX

June 1916

COMMITTEE FOR THE
MEDICAL HISTORY OF THE WAR
Date 31 AUG. 1916

Army Form C. 2118.

WAR DIARY
or
INTELLIGENCE SUMMARY

(Erase heading not required.)

Instructions regarding War Diaries and Intelligence Summaries are contained in F. S. Regs., Part II. and the Staff Manual respectively. Title pages will be prepared in manuscript.

Hour, Date, Place	Summary of Events and Information	Remarks and references to Appendices
1/6/16 to 11/6/16	Routine work at TILQUES R.14. & 9.1 Sheet 27 ASE	"Routine work" is as set out in Vol. III. SRM
12/6/16	Left TILQUES at 9.45 am by road to ST. OMER, entrained 11-40 am, arrived LONGEAUX 9.30 pm. Marched to ALLONVILLE G 11.D Sheet 62.D, arrived 1.50 am. Long with stores proceeded from TILQUES to ALLONVILLE.	SRM SRM
13/6/16 to 27/6/16	Routine work at ALLONVILLE.	SRM
28/6/16	Unit left ALLONVILLE G 11.D Sheet 62.D at 11 am by road, arrived TREAUX J.G.A. Sheet 62.D, arrived 4 pm.	SRM
29/6/16 to 30/6/16	Routine work at TREAUX	SRM

E.P. Matthew Capt. RAMC (T).
O/C 34th Sanitary Sec,
17th Div.

CONFIDENTIAL 17/July

Jy 15/16

34 San Se
vol 10

War Diary
of
34th Sanitary Section
17th Division

From 1st July to 31st July 1916.

Volume X

COMMITTEE FOR THE
MEDICAL HISTORY OF THE WAR
Date 31 AUG 1915

WAR DIARY or INTELLIGENCE SUMMARY

(Erase heading not required.)

Army Form C.2118
SANITARY SECTION
34th
R.A.M.C. (T.)

Hour, Date, Place	Summary of Events and Information	Remarks and references to Appendices
1/7/16 to 5/7/16	Routine work at TREUX. J.6.A.6.D.	" Routine work is as set out in Vol. III. SRM
5/7/16	Shifted position to VILLE E 26 A 1.6	SRM
5/7/16 to 10/7/16	At VILLE. Routine work, including running of Divisional Baths. Cleaning of Streets at VILLE, working of Incinerators at VILLE, and supervision of Burial of dead in the FRICOURT area.	SRM
11/7/16	Left VILLE E 26 by road for CAVILLON	SRM
11/7/16 to 15/7/16	Routine work at CAVILLON	SRM
15/7/16	Left CAVILLON for PONT-REMY	SRM
15/7/16 to 23/7/16	Routine work at PONT-REMY	SRM
23/7/16	Left PONT-REMY for RIBEMONT. J.3.6.6.6. Sheet 62.D.	SRM
23/7/16 to 31/7/16	Routine work at RIBEMONT including running of baths at VILLE for 2 days 26/7/16 and 27/7/16	SRM

S.R Matthews
Capt. R.A.M.C. (T)
O/C 34th Sanitary Sec
17th Div.

August 1916

14th Div.

CONFIDENTIAL 34 San Sec
Vol 11

WAR DIARY
of
34th SANITARY SECTION
17th DIVISION

From 1st August to 31st August 1916

VOLUME XI

COMMITTEE FOR THE
MEDICAL HISTORY OF
Date -5 OCT 1916

Army Form C. 2118.
Medical

WAR DIARY
or
INTELLIGENCE SUMMARY
(Erase heading not required.)

Instructions regarding War Diaries and Intelligence Summaries are contained in F. S. Regs., Part II. and the Staff Manual respectively. Title pages will be prepared in manuscript.

Hour, Date, Place	Summary of Events and Information	Remarks and references to Appendices
1/8/16	Routine work at RIBEMONT	ERM "Routine work" is as set out in my Vol III
2/8/16	Moved to ALBERT E.5.d. 62.D	ERM
3/8/16 to 12/8/16	Routine work at ALBERT.	ERM
13/8/16	Moved to BUIRE D.29.c.55.	ERM
14/8/16	Routine work at BUIRE	ERM
15/8/16	Entrained at MERICOURT for CANDAS. Section marched from CANDAS to BERNAVILLE arrived 4 a.m. Stores and lorry went by road.	ERM
16/8/16	Section marched from BERNAVILLE to DOULLENS. Stores and lorry by road.	ERM
17/8/16	Posted men to duties in new area on relief of 56th Sav. Sanitary Sec. Remainder of Section moved to Hernier Routine work in new area.	ERM ERM ERM
2/1/8/16 to 31/8/16		

/40/1134

11th Div.

No. 34 'Sanitary Section.

Sept. 1916

COMMITTEE FOR THE
MEDICAL HISTORY OF THE WAR
Date   30 OCT. 1916

CONFIDENTIAL

War Diary
of
34th Sanitary Section
17th Divⁿ

From 1st to 30th September 1916

VOLUME X.

WAR DIARY
or
INTELLIGENCE SUMMARY

Army Form C. 2118.

Medical

(Erase heading not required.)

34th SANITARY SECTION — R.A.M.C.(T)

Hour, Date, Place	Summary of Events and Information	Remarks and references to Appendices
1/9/16 to 20/9/16	Routine work at HENU (D19 Sheet 57 D) and Divisional Area including the Sanitation of the villages of HENU, SOUASTRE, MONDICOURT, HALLOY, GRENAS, BENKIERS, SAILLY-AU-BOIS, BAYENCOURT, HEBUTERNE, FONQUEVILLERS, ST AMAND, WARINCOURT, GRINCOURT, GAUDEMPRÉ, PAS. Handed over area to Sanitary Section 33rd Division.	Routine work is as set out in Vol III. The villages of Warincourt, Grincourt were handed over to the Sanitary Sec 9 33rd Division on 12/7/16 SPM
20/9/16		SPM
21/9/16	Section proceeded by road attached to 52nd Inf Bgde to GRENAS bivvy and details direct to St RIQUIER	SPM
22/9/16	Section left GRENAS and arrived at BARLY	SPM
23/9/16	Left BARLY and arrived MAIZICOURT	SPM
24/9/16	Left MAIZICOURT and arrived ST RIQUIER	SPM
25/9/16 to 30/9/16	Routine work at ST RIQUIER and surrounding area	SPM

'40/1617 17

Oct 1916

CONFIDENTIAL

War Diary of
34th Sanitary Section 17th Div'n

From 1st to 31st October 1916

Vol XI

COMMITTEE FOR THE
MEDICAL HISTORY OF THE WAR

Date -9 DEC. 1916

Army Form C. 2118.
MEDICAL

WAR DIARY
INTELLIGENCE SUMMARY
(Erase heading not required.)

Hour, Date, Place	Summary of Events and Information	Remarks and references to Appendices
1/10/16 to 5/10/16	Routine work at ST. RIQUIER — SRM	"Routine work" is as set out in Vol III. SRM
5/10/16	Took over from 49th Divn at PAS — SRM	
6/10/16	Section proceeded by Road to MAISON PONTHIEU attached to 52nd Field Amb. Stores and details proceed derict from ST. RIQUIER to PAS by lorry.	} SRM
7/10/16	Section left MAISON PONTHIEU arrived MEZEROLLES and conveyed from latter place to PAS by motor lorry.	SRM
8/10/16	Posted men to duties in "Divn" Area which included the villages of PAS, (and PAS HUTS), HALLOY, GRENAS, MONDICOURT, and parts of the villages of SOUASTRE, BAYENCOURT, SAILLY-AU-BOIS, and HEBUTERNE —	} SRM
9/10/16 to 20/10/16 21/10/16	Routine work at PAS, and in Divnl Area Duties in above villages taken over by Sanitary Section 48th Divn. Section left PAS, for TREUX by train.	SRM SRM
22/10/16 23 to 26/10/16 27 to 31/10/16 28 to 31/10/16	Temp. work at TREUX by train; stores by motor lorry. SRM Left TREUX for CITADEL (F.21.b. Albert Combined Sheet) SRM Routine work at CITADEL and Divnl Area SRM	

"CONFIDENTIAL"

War Diary of
34th Sanitary Section
From 1st to 30th November 1916.

Vol XX

Army Form C. 2118

WAR DIARY
or
INTELLIGENCE SUMMARY
(Erase heading not required.)

MEDICAL

Instructions regarding War Diaries and Intelligence Summaries are contained in F. S. Regs., Part II. and the Staff Manual respectively. Title pages will be prepared in manuscript.

Hour, Date, Place	Summary of Events and Information	Remarks and references to Appendices
1/11/16 and 2/11/16	Sec to Hdqtrs at CITADEL. F.21.B Albert (Combined Sheet) Routine duties in Area	Routine work is set out in Vol III. SRM
3/11/16	Struck Camp at F.21.B and moved stores and men to MINDEN POST. F.18.C.	SRM — do —
4/11/16 to 14/11/16	Routine duties in Divisional Area	SRM — do —
15/11/16	Struck Camp at F.18.C. and proceeded with men and stores by lorry to Rest Area. Sec to Hdqtrs at RIENCOURT	SRM
16/11/16 to 25/11/16	Routine duties in Rest Area, including the sanitation of the following villages:— CAVILLON, PICQUIGNY, OISSY, MOLLIENS-VIDAME, CAMPS-EN-AMIENOIS, MONTAGNE, SOUES, LE MESGE, RIENCOURT, ST. PIERRE, AILLY-SUR-SOMME, BREILLY, SAISSEMONT, SAUSSEVAL. ditto	SRM — do —
26/11/16 to 30/11/16	ditto	

17
140/1903
1/Div.

CONFIDENTIAL Vol/5

WAR DIARY
of
34th Sanitary Section

From 1st to 31st Dec 1916

VOL. XIII

COMMITTEE FOR THE
MEDICAL HISTORY OF THE WAR
Date 31 JAN. 1917

34th SANITARY SECTION — R.A.M.C.T.

WAR DIARY or INTELLIGENCE SUMMARY

Army Form C. 2118.

(Erase heading not required.)

Hour, Date, Place	Summary of Events and Information	Remarks and references to Appendices
1/12/16 to 12/12/16	Routine duties in Div^l Area including Sanitation of the following villages:— CAVILLON, PICQUIGNY, OISY, MOLLIENS-VIDAME, CAMPS-en-AMIENOIS, MONTAINE, SOUES, la-MESGE, RIENCOURT, ST. PIERRE, AILLY-sur-SOMME, BREILLY, SAISSEMONT, SAUSSEVAL and FOURDRINOY. Plans were prepared of each of these villages, and the Sanitation greatly improved. Section and Stores moved from RIENCOURT, and took over at CORBIE.	ERM. ERM.
13/12/16	Handed over TRAINING AREA No 3 to San Sec^t 29th Div, and established system of Sanitary Supervision in CORBIE. While occupying this "RESERVE Area" many sanitary improvements were carried out by the 17th Div including the erection of several public latrines, public urinals, incinerators and other useful structures in CORBIE, and new latrines, urinals, and incinerators in the villages in the Area. The R.E.'s did much useful work in this direction.	ERM. ERM.
14/12/16	O/C proceeded to FORWARD AREA, and took over the BATHS and SANITATION from San Sec^t 20th Div. Section and Stores moved to "FORWARD AREA". Routine work in "FORWARD AREA" including Baths work	

24/1/12/16
25/12/16 to
31/12/16

140/1943

14th Div.

CONFIDENTIAL

War Diary of 34th Sanitary Section
From 1st to 31st January 1917

Volume — XIV

COMMITTEE FOR THE
MEDICAL HISTORY OF THE WAR
Date 13 MAR. 1917

WAR DIARY
INTELLIGENCE SUMMARY

(Erase heading not required.)

Medical

Hour, Date, Place	Summary of Events and Information	Remarks and references to Appendices
1/1/17 to 15/1/17	Routine duties in Forward Area i.e. Sec. Hofton at A² d.9.1 "Albert Combine" Sheet. Sanitary Supervision of CARNOY. HUTS AREA and GUILLEMONT. Supervision of Water Points at CARNOY, COSY CORNER, GUILLEMONT, TALUS BOISE.	ERM
16/1/17	Handed over Area to San Sec 29th Div, and proceeded with men and stores by Motor lorry to CORBIE, and took over from San Sec 29th Div.	ERM
17/1/17 to 27/1/17	Routine duties in CORBIE, and supervision of sanitation in the following villages:— CORBIE, BONNAY, LAHOUSSAYE, VILLE, part of MEAULTE, and MERICOURT L'ABBE —	ERM
28/1/17	Left CORBIE and took over Forward Area Sect. Hofton at MINDEN POST F.1.B.C (Albert Combine Sheet). Polled men to duty at COMBLES, MALTZ HORN CAMP and BRONFAY FARM CAMPS	ERM
29/1/17 to 31/1/17	Routine duties in Forward Area	ERM

11th Div.

CONFIDENTIAL. Vol 77

14/1/1917

WAR DIARY OF

34TH. SANITARY SECTION.

FROM 1ST to 28TH. FEBY. 1917.

VOLUME XI.

COMMITTEE FOR THE
MEDICAL HISTORY OF THE WAR

Date 4 — APR. 1917

Feb. 1917

WAR DIARY
INTELLIGENCE SUMMARY

34th SANITARY SECTION R.A.M.C.(T)

Hour, Date, Place	Summary of Events and Information	Remarks and references to Appendices
1/2/17 to 20/2/17	Section Hdqtrs at MINDEN POST, F18.C (Albert Combined Sheet). Routine duties in forward Area, including Sanitary supervision and improvements at BRONFAY FARM Camps, MALTZHORN CAMP, COMBLES and HAIE WOOD. Supervision of Water supplies in COMBLES, and control of Gum-boot drying Stores.	S.R.M.
21/2/17	Handed over "forward Area" to Sanitary Section 29th Division. Portion of Section proceeded to HEILLY, and took over the Area from San? Sec. 29th Division. Motor lorry Stores, and portion of Section detained at MINDEN POST in consequence of New Restrictions.	S.R.M.
22/2/17 to 28/2/17	Routine work in Area, including Sanitary supervision and improvements in the various villages in the Area, including HEILLY, MEAULTE, FRANVILLERS, LA HOUSSOYE, DAOURS, BONNAY, BUSSY and LA NEUVILLE.	S.R.M.

17

17th Div.

140/2043

Vol 18

CONFIDENTIAL.

WAR DIARY OF

34th SANITARY SECTION

from 1st to 31st MARCH 1917.

VOLUME XVI

COMMITTEE FOR THE
MEDICAL HISTORY OF THE WAR
Date 11 MAY. 1917

Army Form C. 2118

WAR DIARY
INTELLIGENCE SUMMARY
(Erase heading not required.)

Place	Date	Hour	Summary of Events and Information	Remarks and references to Appendices
HEILLY	1/3/17	—	Location of Section Headquarters. Four of the personnel left HEILLY with a portion of the Section Stores and reported at CONTAY.	
CONTAY	2/3/17	—	Remainder of Personnel of Section Headquarters proceeded to CONTAY.	
"	3/3/17 to 9/3/17	—	Supervision of the sanitation of the following villages in the Reserve Area, taken over, viz;— CONTAY, WARLOY, RUBEMPRÉ, HERISSART, and PUCHEVILLERS, and routine sanitary duties carried out in these villages.	
"	10/3/17	9 a.m.	Orders received from A.P.M.S. 17th Div: for the whole of the personnel & stores of the Section to proceed at once to TALMAS, and to take over the sanitary supervision of the Southern Staging Area under the D.D.M.S. XIII Corps.	
TALMAS	10/3/17	5 p.m.	Arrived at TALMAS, and established Sanitary Section Headquarters.	

Army Form C. 2118

WAR DIARY
INTELLIGENCE SUMMARY
(Erase heading not required.)

Place	Date	Hour	Summary of Events and Information	Remarks and references to Appendices
TALMAS	11/3/17		O/c visited D.D.M.S. XIII Corps at DOULLENS, and arranged details in regard to the sanitary supervision of the TALMAS and MOLLIENS-AU-BOIS Staging areas.	
"	12/3/17		Inspection made of the villages of TALMAS, NAOURS, WARGNIES, and HAVERNAS.	
"	13/3/17		A party of the Personnel left Section Headquarters to take up sanitary duties at MOLLIENS-AU-BOIS, and the following villages viz, PIERREGOT, MIRVAUX, RAINNEVILLE, and SEPTENVILLE.	
"	14/3/17		O/c inspected MOLLIENS-AU-BOIS.	
"	15/3/17 to 18/3/17		Routine Sanitary duties carried out in the two Staging areas of TALMAS and MOLLIENS-AU-BOIS.	
	19/3/17		Notified by D.D.M.S XIII Corps, that Corps is leaving the Area, & that in future all reports & returns from the Section are to be sent direct to D.M.S Fifth Army.	

Army Form C. 2118.

WAR DIARY
INTELLIGENCE SUMMARY

(Erase heading not required.)

Hour, Date, Place	Summary of Events and Information	Remarks and references to Appendices
20/3/17 TALMAS	O/c 35th Sanitary Section asked for reliefs to be sent to the villages of HERISSART, HARPONVILLE, WARLOY and CONTAY. Personnel from this Section sent as reliefs on this date.	
21/3/17 TALMAS	Personnel sent to take charge of the sanitary supervision of RUBEMPRE and PUCHEVILLERS.	
22/3/17 "	Two of the Personnel posted to the Divisional Artillery Staging Area, for the supervision of the sanitation of ST LEGER and ST OUEN.	
23/3/17 "	O/c visited LAVICOGNE, NAOURS, & FLEXELLES.	
24/3/17 "	O/c visited MOLLIENS-AU-BOIS & HERISSART.	
25/3/17 "	O/c granted special leave of one month from 26-3-17 to 26-4-17. O/c 71st San Sec. to take charge of area during absence of O/c 35th San Sec	11/3

Army Form C. 2118.

WAR DIARY
INTELLIGENCE SUMMARY

(Erase heading not required.)

Instructions regarding War Diaries and Intelligence
Summaries are contained in F. S. Regs., Part II.
the Staff Manual respectively. Title pages
be prepared in manuscript.

Hour, Date, Place	Summary of Events and Information	Remarks and references to Appendices
26/3/17. TALMAS.	O/c 71st San. Sec: visited this Sam.Sec: Headquarters. Inspection made of the villages of WARLOY & CONTAY.	1/2"
27/3/17 "	Constructional work in regard to the provision of four public latrines in TALMAS completed	1/2"
28/3/17 " to 31/3/17 "	Routine sanitary work carried out in the staging Areas and in the villages in the Eastern Area.	1/2"

[signature] Army Dept: R.A.M.C.(T)
for O.C. 34 San Sec;

www.ingramcontent.com/pod-product-compliance
Lightning Source LLC
Chambersburg PA
CBHW081451160426
43193CB00013B/2439